THE SUGAR·BABY
BIBLE
By Eden Carpenter

THE SUGAR·BABY
BIBLE

Copyright 2019

ACKNOWLEDGEMENTS:
*I would like to express my undying love
and GRATITUDE to my Daddies who
brought me to where I am today.
Because of my Daddies' love and protection
my life is comfortable, secure and beautiful.
These men have so generously contributed
to my success as a woman
and my Gratitude is eternal.*

THE SUGAR·BABY
BIBLE
BY EDEN CARPENTER

TABLE OF CONTENTS

INTRODUCTION

In the beginning, there was only darkness with no living creatures upon the Earth and no light upon the Earth. God said, "Let there be light," and there was light. God saw that it was GOOD. Let there be Sugar Babies and Sugar Daddies. He saw it was Good. Let this light shine on a Secret Society Lifestyle, and it, too, was GOOD.

Then, over the millennia, planets and comets and all that spun around in space coalesced into the galaxies and the universe, and it was GOOD.

On one of these planets, because it was special and chosen, there came to be creatures of the sea, air and land, plants in uncountable numbers and the most special of all creatures, a Sugar Baby and a Sugar Daddie, and they dwelt in paradise. God saw it was GOOD.

The Sugar Babies and Sugar Daddies were given dominion over all the earth, the plants, and the animals and were told they could partake of all the wonders therein, except they must not eat from the tree at the center of the garden, but the serpent deceived the Sugar Baby and she ate of the fruit of knowledge and then persuaded her Sugar Daddie to do likewise, because Daddie will do whatever his Sugar Baby suggests. Since they both ate of the forbidden fruit of knowledge, they were banned from paradise and their lives became as difficult as it is today.

Now, we find ourselves still suffering from this ban from a paradise we should have had. We have lackluster careers, we have faithless marriages, we have unmanageable bills, we have loneliness, and we have little if any guidance from other loving humans. We treat ourselves poorly. We don't respect ourselves. We continually demean ourselves. We sell ourselves short. WE are a mess. It's time to take control of our lives and become what we envision ourselves to be and what we truly are meant to be.

As it has been written, "We must love our

neighbors as ourselves." So it shall be done. The key part in that statement is, "as ourselves." We must love ourselves BEFORE we can love others. The first step towards loving ourselves is RESPECT. We respect ourselves by doing only things that elevate us from the crowd. We stop the physical abuse to our bodies. We treat our bodies like the Temples they were meant to be; no poison enters the Temple, no evil thoughts enter the Temple, no evil actions enter the Temple. We must purify and honor our Temple.

The following pages will help you to purify and build your Temple, they will spell out the way to become what you really want to be: a fulfilled Sugar Baby who controls her own destiny, a person who is happy and healthy… a true woman of contentment. In other words, a true Sugar Baby.

The very concept of having or being a Sugar Baby is controversial, to say the least, but let's get real; society's rules are not applicable to each and every one of us in our diverse lifestyles today. We live in an era where Bruce

Jenner, the All American-USA Olympian, was featured on every box of Wheaties, who is now Caitlyn Jenner – a woman. Strong, well muscled men are patting the butts in a much-too-friendly way of their football playing buddies, making all taboos head for the exits. Gorgeous movie stars like Madonna and Brittany Spears making out on the TV screen, sending confusing messages to our impressionable girls and the public worldwide. So, needless to say, this is the time to confront the stigma surrounding the Sugar Daddie and Sugar Baby concept AND its many misconceptions.

You may wonder why so many marriages fail and why more and more are not even happening these days. Some of us are not really equipped to be in lifelong monogamous relationships. A traditional relationship provides its own challenges whether it is the possibility of cheating, dealing with baby daddy/momma drama, the ever-present in-laws, jealous friends who sabotage your love life, all of the social media circus today, or abuse in any capacity. The list is endless.

In a Sugar Baby/Sugar Daddies relationship you can disregard almost all of that entirely (and hereafter, for simplicity we will refer Sugar Baby/Sugar Daddies as SB/SD).

There are no rules that bind you to the other. You would almost never say to Daddies or Baby: "Do not do this… do not do that or else," because then you are certainly not in a SB/SB relationship; you are in fact in a real society-driven relationship that statistically lasts less than fifty percent of the time. Daddies and Babies are free to do as they please. This freedom is like a playground. I will explain that in more detail later on in the Bible. "This is the unspoken secret."

It is so obvious, by the rate of divorces and the lack of marriages even taking place today, and the infidelity that is rampant, that there are other solutions to relationship, friendship, and love; Men being Women, Women being Men, Girl/Girl, Boy/Boy, and accordingly SB/SD or whatever floats your boat…. let's not waste any more time, and get to it!

THE TEN COMMANDMENTS OF THE SUGAR BABY BIBLE

1-THOU SHALT NEVER exchange sex for money • Doing that makes you a prostitute. Prostitutes are not SugarBabies!

2-THOU SHALT NEVER reveal your real name or address • Wait until much later in relationship, when you are comfortable and trust has been fully established.

3-THOU SHALT NEVER entertain your Daddies at your home • This is a Cardinal rule you NEVER break. Your home is your safe place, your haven, and should never be compromised.

4-THOU SHALT NEVER have intimacy on the first date • Or have any other intimacies on first meeting. This meeting is to determine if you have any chemistry with this man and does he meet your standards and requirements. Be classy.

**5-THOU SHALT NEVER get drunk in
public or on the first encounter** • Act digni-
fied, like the Sugar Baby you are claiming to
be.

**6-THOU SHALT meet in public the first en-
counter** • You should leave after a maximum
of 1-hour limit because you are a busy Baby.
Always leave him wanting more.

**7-THOU SHALT ALWAYS LOOK LIKE
THE Sugar Baby YOU ARE** • Apply tasteful makeup. Look like a million. Always fix
your hair and do your nails. Smell alluring and
mysterious. Always wear elegant but appropriate clothes - a simple yet slightly flirty dress is
always a good idea.

**8-THOU SHALT ALWAYS SMILE. Let
a smile be your umbrella** • Be happy. Be
his world away from his worries. Be his safe
place to hide. Be his joy from the storm.

**9-THOU SHALT NEGOTIATE
BEFOREHAND. Have the details all fig-
ured out BEFORE you commit** •

Remember, no sugar goes out of the sugar bowl until the sugar bowl has been filled.

10-THOU SHALT ALWAYS be private and discrete • Never tell anybody what you are doing, or with whom. Discretion is! Safety and security is what being a Sugar Baby is all about.

GENESIS:
THE BEGINNING
So you want to be a Sugar Baby.

Get comfortable; grab a snack and have your iphone and note pad ready, because I have the tea, Baby. The most important thing you need to do, is do EXACTLY what I tell you. This is the Bible, after all. Amen.

I know you dream of perfectly manicured nails, lush shiny hair, designer labels, foreign cars, shopping sprees and global travel. You want the fantasy you dream of or you would not have picked up this Bible. I am proof you can have it all. But there are things you should do and things you should NEVER do: above all, keep The Ten Commandments of the Sugar Baby Bible.

I come from nothing, even less than nothing. My biological Daddy was a gang lord, convicted felon, and then a born again preacher, and had nothing financially to provide for me or my family… not even a home. You better believe one needs a stable financial livelihood to live, flourish and to become a successful individual in our society, and who can contribute in a positive, healthy way to this beautiful planet we call home. Being alive is FUCKING expensive, Babies.

I made a decision as a young girl that I was not going to live and suffer and continue to go without as an adult the same way I was forced to endure as a child and teenager. When I was not under the control of my husband, fiancé, or boyfriend and I was finally free to choose what was best for me, I was able to flourish into the Perfect Sugar Baby that I am today.

Being in a SB/SD relationship is a Real and Genuine Relationship, not your conventional type, but a REAL relationship. You are NOT a prostitute; you DO NOT have sex for money!! Ever!! I have seen interviews of young women and men "claiming" to be a Sugar Babies but they could not hold their ground during the question and answer interviews, literally embarrassing themselves and our SB/SD lifestyle in Sugarland. They took the idea of money that they were desperate for and convoluted it with earning a living. They were ignorant and did not know how to manage themselves accordingly, breaking ALL of The Ten Commandments.

If you are serious about being a Sugar Baby there is specific information you must know and accept; Daddies are rich, financially comfortable and secure, educated and smart. You can play naive, but don't *be* naive.

First of all, understand you will need their mentoring. If you go into this or any relationship with the attitude of human hijacking or manipulation by violating the natural laws of the universe, you will lose. Vise versa if the potential Daddie is solely in it for manipulation and sex in exchange for money, he is the real prostitute. GTFO, Babies, QUICKLY! That is NO Daddie.

The process of weeding out the frauds and fakes is an art I have mastered, and after 15 plus years I am ready to put my stamp on the rules and share The Ten Commandments of

this relationship because I have found it to be
the only one that actually works.

Keep in mind this relationship is not for ev-
eryone. The marriage concept is not for me; a
cheating BF/GF relationship is not for me, the
relationships in the LGBT community are not
for me, however, you will never see or hear
me judge any of it, because this is about love,
comfort and security. We all choose every day.
We all have the gift of freewill and as long as
you harm no one, including yourself, do as
you please. Judgment is for God only.
Respect others, ALWAYS.

If you lack a strong moral fiber and deprive
yourself of seeking higher education, close
this little Bible and be on your way, an
attitude of self-righteousness will sabotage
you immediately. Ignorance will hang you. If
you want to be a teacher, go to college and get
your degree. If you want to be a cosmetolo-
gist, go to beauty school. You get the picture?
If you want to be a true Sugar Baby, this is the
Bible you need, Babies. This is not about one
way to do it; it's the only way. It is the yellow

brick road to the sweet life in the Paradise of Sugarland.

ECCLESIASTICS: BE CLASSY.
Exactly what is Sugar?

"SUGARING", in case you're new to this sweet life or simply curious, is a type of lifestyle where a "Sugar Baby" provides companionship in exchange for being pampered, while a "Sugar Daddie" pampers Sugar Babies in return for companionship. "Pampering" is obviously a nebulous term, and can include explicitly negotiated financial amounts — like an allowance, tuition payments or an investment into a Sugar Baby's business venture, or simply gifts, trips, and other treats. "Companionship" is an equally broad term, which can range from private recess, to casual dating, to a monogamous relationship, to being a married Daddie's extra partner, and quite often his preferred one.

A "Sugar Relationship" is defined as a "Sugar Daddie" who provides mentoring and/or financial assistance to a Sugar Baby." Often this is a colloquial way to describe an arrangement.

A Sugar Relationship is based on the degree to which a Sugar Daddie agrees to take care of a Sugar Baby, which is typically proportional to Sugar Daddie's net worth and how often he/she wants to see his Sugar Baby. The sugar relationship can take on many forms; the length of the relationship, the duration of dates, the frequency of dates, and the goals of both the Sugar Daddie and the Sugar Baby.

This might be time for a refresher course in the definitions of "SUGAR". Most are quick to label the Sugar lifestyle choice as prostitution, but there are many differences between this lifestyle and the oldest profession in the world. High-end or not, a call girl is NOT another word for a Sugar Baby!

A Relationship vs. A Transaction
A prostitute and a client have a "transactional" relationship. They meet, exchange money, and participate in some sort of physical act and then part ways. Typically, this is a one-time occurrence… a perfunctory job. There is and will be no relationship. That is the key difference really: no ongoing relationship.

Being a Sugar Baby vs. Being a Prostitute
SUGAR is a lifestyle choice, not a profession. A Sugar Baby is a woman who wants to date financially secure men who can provide her with the lifestyle she desires. She's selective about whom she dates; a prostitute isn't picky who her clients are.

Dating a Sugar Baby vs. Hiring a Prostitute
A Sugar Daddie is generous, and wants to see their partner succeed. When two people are involved in a mutually beneficial relationship, they respect and value one another's time. Sugar relationships can turn into long-term serious relationships. Prostitutes are paid to perform a service. A john doesn't want a hooker to stick around, and a Sugar Daddie doesn't want his Sugar Baby to leave. A Sugar Daddie will take his Baby to Greece for a week or even to the Kentucky Derby to be with his friends, so he must enjoy her company and be proud of her beauty and charm.

Quality vs. Quantity
Most Sugar Babies aren't totally immersed in the sugar world. Sugar Babies are also teach-

ers, college students, actresses, and business professionals. They look for successful mentors that can further their career, not just a temporary fix.

Prostitutes use their trade as a source of income — it's a last resort for many women who are short on cash. They aren't looking for mentors or anyone with a specific level of expertise. One might meet hundreds of prostitutes before finding anyone to fulfill your emotional needs. Prostitutes are hired to be whomever you want them to be, but they won't necessarily be themselves. She treats you like a job, not like a Daddie.

"Sugar" for Daddie is clearly a HOT, delicious sweet arm candy, passion, a sincerely beautifully polished Baby who needs mentoring and is completely playful. For the Babies, it is CASH, CASH and more CASH. "Cash" is plastic, cars, designer labels, splurges, your home, higher education, your own business… whatever your heart desires and mentoring and support on many levels. The financial fortitude that provides peace of mind and stability that no 9-5 job could ever provide you with. Why? Because your days and time are spent focusing on your dreams and goals… the things that lift you up and make you a better you, Baby .

First, call out the posers, so many wannabees think they can "hook up" with a Beautiful Baby, but if you don't know **The Ten Commandments of the Sugar Baby Bible** and you "think" you have an idea of what a SB is, you will quickly find yourself used, taken advantage of and forgotten! No Daddie is going to respect and care of you or provide for you longer than one night if you don't respect yourself. Make sure you use this Bible for a step-by-step guide to becoming an exclusive Sugar Baby.

In this day and age of social media with sites like; BackPage, the local me-so-horny spas on every corner, strip clubs with their private rooms, why should a discerning man or woman want or need to provide for a SB? Therein is the difference; you're not a prostitute. You are to be adored, cherished, provided and cared for, and you are a treasure to Daddie just like his portfolio, his Rolls Royce, his Rolex watch, and just like his other valuable property, you have immense VALUE. Quite honestly, the real discerning, discriminating Daddies will not settle for anything less than the Best.

If you want cheap, you will get cheap. Cheap always breaks, Baby. An authentic SD wants a playful, classy, easy on the eyes solid 10. Sugar for SD is their kryptonite. They are not going to support a train wreck; by that I mean, if you have an issue with alcohol, drugs, you're not polished in your overall appearance, you have no career or higher education goals, no focus for your future, or have a foul mouth, etc., you know what and who you are Baby, keep it moving… this Lifestyle is not for you! Please seek help for any addictions. No two-bit messy, foul-mouthed unfocused individual will be financed to a discerning lifestyle. If you cannot function in the capacity I just describe, a SD is not going to transform you from the ground up.

Please be educated or on a path to higher education with ambition. Be book smart/

street smart, be classy, be kind, be playful and SMILE, Darling. Being a Sugar Baby is a "blow-your-mind kind of secret society" that Daddie can't get anywhere else.

An authentic SD is not greedy, stingy, or demeaning to you. They have plenty of sugar and want to spoil their Baby with lavish spending to keep them happy, content and playful. That is what keeps them coming back. Sugar is what all Babies want, our taste is sweet, "I need Sugar, Daddie."

Why would you, as a bona fide SB share your PRICELESS commodity; your face, body, mind, soul, dreams to just anyone, if they are not taking excellent care of you?

If you do not value yourself, how can anyone else? Ask yourself, why are you in a relationship with a loser, a cheater… someone who disrespects you and does not pay your bills? Any well-gained asset is thoroughly thought out, planned for and hard work and purpose put in. So, PUT IN yourself! Sugar will sustain your life and keep you on an even track so you can complete your education or create that business, so you can focus on positive things and rise to higher levels in society.

DEUTERONOMY: DO RIGHT BY ME
How and where does a SD/SM meet a SB?

Today there are discerning web sites for this and your profile must match accordingly. Your profile includes a few tastefully selected photos, a description of yourself and your needs (clearly spelled out). Let's start with your photos, then to your profile description:

Please, please, please do not look like a trashy, messy unpolished person. Smile and shine brightly, like a diamond.

Do not include other people in your photo. He wants to see you, not your best friend, children or even pets. Your Starbucks coffee cup or iPhone is okay.

Make sure the main photo is a head and shoulders portrait-style photo. Be confident and **SMILE**. He doesn't want a solemn sour puss. The other pictures in your series should hint at

any or all of your charms… up to a point. No
sense giving away all the goodies. There is a
tasteful, and I do mean mouth-watering tasteful way to project you to any possible Daddie.
All our cellular phones are equipped with
cameras that have timers, and great Photoshop
apps out there… make use of them. No Snapchat filters, Ewe! Daddie wants the real you.
Like his Bentley or his Rolex!

You must do your hair, your make up, plan an
elegant sexy outfit with accessories of plush
pillows, silk or jewelry that exemplify wealth,
and then pose Baby, pose. Strike a Vogue.
Ride your bike, hold flowers, run on the beach,
sip champagne, stand in front of expensive
cars, read a book, and enjoy your Starbucks
cappuccino. Take beautiful photos and keep
your photos updated. Men are visual and love
to look at you. Keep yourself polished. Think
of your photos as a "visual" profile. Let your
photos describe what and who you are, and
what possible heavenly delights anyone who
might be selected, can expect to enjoy.
Your written profile should include specific
things about yourself such as height, age, city

or and race, what you like to do with your life, your hobbies and an interesting fact about you.

BUT you are NOT suggesting what you want for your allowance! You are searching here. The agreed upon allowance amount is for AFTER the meeting when you know that there is chemistry and a certain level of trust. This is a platform to attract the right long-term Daddie.

NUMBERS:
STEP-BY-STEP.
Time to Meet.

So, you have been contacted by many sup-
plicants and after reading all they have to say,
you choose one or more to be considered. In
these "before meeting" discussions, NEVER
discuss money or the allowance. Reserve that
until after you decide if the
prospective Daddie is worthy of your atten-
tions. After a few messages are exchanged,
you decide to meet to see if any of them fit
your parameters or how much, if any, chemistry is there. Remember, this is NOT a date or
a one-time thing you're seeking, it's a long-
term commitment with all of the luxuries only
a true Sugar Daddie can shower you with. This
is an interview, for both of you. Be charming,
beautiful, alluring, and be playful. Ideally he
doesn't get to choose,
you do.

Be yourself. Brush up on current events so
that you can have conversations that are intel-

lectually stimulating. Of course, your charm
and appearance are very important, but you
need to be the whole package – beauty, brains,
and charm. Teach yourself a joke. Be witty.

THE COMMANDMENTS OF ENGAGEMENT FOR MEETINGS

These and all of the Commandment must NEVER be broken. Always Meet in Public… REPEAT… ALWAYS MEET IN PUBLIC… like at a coffee shop, a bistro or classy local restaurant for a cocktail. If you choose a cocktail, sip, don't finish and don't order a second one. Ice tea with lemon is perfect.

DO NOT GET DRUNK… keep yourself together, Baby. You are here to change your life, not fuck it up. I have seen this so many times; you're looking beautiful and polished and you get a few cocktails in and forget yourself. Oh no, future Daddie is watching you, sizing you up and judging you. This is not a night at the club. This is not an opportunity to indulge in a complimentary drink and start confessing your woes and worries and be sloppy. This is your potential Daddie and you want him to protect you and provide for you and respect you like he respects all of his other valuables. Have your cocktail, if you must, but sip and do not finish it entirely. There is a time and place for drinking adult beverages but this is an interview. Instead, choose a flavored ice tea, a cappuccino, a coke, anything, or limit yourself to one drink. You do not EVER drink and drive either!

Keep it short. You have someplace to be right after. You are an exclusive Baby on the way to her goals and dreams, keep this meeting short and sweet, you are valuable, and believe me, Daddie will be texting you as soon and you blow a kiss and walk out the door. Don't forget to blow the kiss, NOT give a real one. Flirty is fun. A seasoned Daddie knows what he is looking for and he knows if you know the ropes too. Keep the initial meeting short, no longer than (1) HOUR, keep him wanting more, even Daddie knows time is money!!

NEVER, EVER go to his house or a hotel and sleep with him on the first meeting, no matter how much he offers! Because if you do, that just makes you a prostitute! You are not qualified for the Sugar Baby lifestyle, and you want more than that. You want to be his Sugar Baby.

Wear an outfit that fits you properly. Make sure it is clean, pretty and playful, but a bit conservative, Baby. Visuals are always best to draw from. You could be going to yoga or spin class right after in a sexy outfit fashioned with a jacket you will slide off at the appropriate time. Keep control of the situation. A dress is always a perfect idea, always. Please wear perfume or body spray and make sure your nails are polished, your hair clean and in a nice beautiful hairstyle, down or up. Make sure your teeth are whitened and clean. As long as you feel confident and finish with a cheerful attitude and a million dollar smile, the rest is a cake walk down the yellow brick road to Sugarland.

Be happy even if you have to fake it. Happiness is contagious, and after all, that's what Daddie wants: a happy, beautiful escape from his routine and predictable life. Do not lead with your needs and wants. You are not des-

perate, even though you may be underneath
it all (your charm will solve all those issues
quite easily and quickly). Be so enticing and
sweet that SD will ask you what you want and
need. As long as you follow the Ten Commandments of Sugar Baby Bible, your needs
will be met and fulfilled until it overflows.
I promise.

FIRST CORINTHIANS:
Time to Negotiate

If you have gotten this far, and it can take time for this to happen with the right SD, or it can happen quite fast… you are on your way. Remember, you are in control, always.

The Allowance:
Daddie will or should offer an allowance. At that time it should be established: when and how much is to be deposited into your account. Allowances are on a monthly schedule, never a per visit experience… that's what prostitutes do. Daddie will have a plan, this is true with most successful men. Both of you are on a trial period here. This is prime time to keep control of this situation. Tell your Daddie that he is on a trial period for 30 days to see how things go for each of you. This should provide comfort and you both will be on your best behavior. If both of you are happy and things work out and progress, this will be the reward for all of your persistent and dedicated hard work.

Boundaries:
Each one of us has limits and boundaries. Be sure both of yours are clear. If you don't want to have physical intimacy at all, say so. Be sure that's what he wants the relationship to entail as well before any agreement is made. Clear understandings are critical here. Be sure and let him know that no amount of abuse or control, is EVER acceptable

Where to meet for get-togethers or as I like to call it: Recess.
A get-together or recess can take place anywhere, but remember Commandment #3, never entertain your Daddie in your home. Always go to a hotel or to his home, office, yacht, or restaurants, but NEVER in your home. Your home is your safe place, your refuge, your haven… and should never be a playground for recess.

How long should a recess last?
Establish a time frame in which your recess should occur. And they can take many forms: fun lunch/dinner engagement or a trip that is planned in advance. Flexibility and mutual re-

spect of each other's responsibilities are paramount and this will create a bond between you both. Essentially recess is determined by both of your schedules and is flexible.

How often should you meet each month?
This is quite often the most difficult thing to arrange. Life happens and schedules change, it may be difficult to satisfy all the things that can alter your plans. It is best to schedule the same time and place for all of your recesses, but that does take away from spontaneity, which believe me, is the spice of life. However, it is always best to know how many times each week or month you will meet. Agree on that and stick to it. Be sure and keep a calendar or diary and record your actions… not like a tell-all book, but just for record keeping. Because, trust me, Daddie is keeping track.

A relationship is always changing. Life is always changing. This is when the relationship takes on deeper levels.

ACTS:
ACT RIGHT, BABY. Recess

You have arrived, Baby. SUGARLAND

Remember when you were a child in school and it was time for recess? You may have wondered why I was using this term in 1st Corinthians, well, here's why: who doesn't look forward to recess? My point is… be playful and help the pressures of day-to-day life disappear. Boys chase girls, girls chase boys, all the toys on the playground, yes, Babies play. Turn on Katy Perry's "Teenage Dream," dance around, wear playful outfits, giggle and jiggle, tell funny stories, suck lollipops, eat cotton candy or make a bikini out of it. Be your playful, invigorating and addicting self. No matter what is going on in your life, your time together is always limited, so make the very most of it.

Find a fun playful name to call Daddie when you are at recess. It can be Uncle Daddie, Big Daddie, Daddie BooBoo, or Money, I mean

Honey. You get the drift. Be sincere in all you do. Create that bond in a place where you both can go safely. You are one another's safe, fun, carefree retreat. It's best not to flaunt this relationship; privacy is paramount, because some Daddies are married. Remember, to always make healthy choices for yourself.

You are a Sugar Baby. Daddie looks forward to his recess time with you because there is no drama, no bullshit, and just before recess is when you sit on Daddie's lap and tell him all the things you need in life, which are outside of the allowance. Sit on his lap,
caress his hair, look into his eyes, and confess sweetly… "Daddie, this happened. And I need you." He will come to your rescue because, afterall, isn't that what Daddies do?

RECESS is whatever you BOTH want it to be, and sometimes, it's nothing but cuddling and being together, because he just wants to be near you and away from everything else. You are his Baby, after all. Make him feel like there is NOWHERE else he would rather be. Not all Sugar Baby relationships require physical intimacy because intimacy is many things. The options are endless honestly.

Your relationship is your own, make your own recess rules. Your private life is that, it is your private life.

Recess is Sugar. This is what it's all about, for both Baby and Daddie. Please keep an open mind here, do not be greedy, be grateful and playful. This will be the yellow brick road to Sugarland. Listen, be yourself, be playful and fun. This relationship does not work like a marriage or dating your ex's. This is Sugarland, Baby. It's sweet, mouthwatering and most of all fucking satisfying for both of you. Indulge. The keys to your lavish or comfortable, worry-free lifestyle will be found in RECESS. The way you word everything and how you use your words are so important, when dealing with Daddie, your playtime is RECESS, and RECESS is spelled S-U-G-A-R.

KEEP THREE THINGS PRIVATE:

1-Your income

2-Your personal life

3-Your Daddie!

In closing, I shall remain anonymous because society is hypocritical and this is my choice.

May all your fantasies come to life.

Love, Thee Sugar Baby.

The Ten Commandments
for taking
a good profile picture.

1-Have at least one close-up, portrait-style
photo. Let him see the real you.
And smile, Baby, smile.

2-Be alone in your picture. Do NOT include
pets or friends. He wants to see only YOU.

3-Wear simple, yet classy clothes, with
appropriate accessories. Time to break out the
Gucci, Fendi, Versace, Louis Vuitton.

4-Be classy. Dress fun, but not silly, and no
Snapchat filters!

5-Be flirty and provocative, but this is NOT a
Playboy spread. Don't give away all of your
secrets. Leave him wanting more.

6-Do not cover your face with sunglasses or a
big floppy hat. Remember, your face is your
fortune.

7-Make sure the picture is in focus and properly exposed, and I don't mean more cleavage, please.

8-Be creative with the location of your picture: take it at the beach, the museum, the park, or standing beside a Mercedes.

9-First and foremost, smile. Or at least be pleasant, neutral, or provocative. Do NOT scowl or do "duck-lips". That may be fine for Facebook or Snapchat. But honey, now you're after bigger game.

10-Have your hair and make-up done in every photo, maybe in different styles, showing all the wonderful looks you can achieve.

SUGAR NOTES

55